H
Onto
Hope

By
Patricia Rose

Published by Patricia Rose

Text by Patricia Rose. Copyright 2010

Cover Photograph by Kate Howe. Copyright 2010

Printed by Creative Digital Printing. Shrewsbury. U.K.

ISBN: 978-0-9562629-2-9

Previous Titles;
Words of Comfort (by Patricia Rose) 2009
Every One A Hero (by Patricia Rose) 2009

Introduction

I was inspired to write this little book because whatever age, race or religion you are, we all need hope. Hope is like the sun, the more it shines the more lives it touches.

Whatever you may be going through in your life, and whatever problems you may be facing, a few words of hope and inspiration can make all the difference as to how you view things. It can open your heart and mind to a more positive way of thinking.

As you read through these poems I hope and pray you will be inspired to face the future with hope in your heart, and with a belief that dreams really can come true.

From my heart
to yours

Patricia Rose

Contents

Contents *-continued*

Hope

Hope is like a letter
That's coming through the post,
It hasn't yet arrived
But it's what you look for most.

It could hold all the answers
To a dream you've had for years,
It could hold out a promise –
Or it could confirm your fears.

But as long as it's still coming
You know that you can cope,
You know you can keep going
As long as there is hope.

Hope for the Future

Each year we wait for midnight
To arrive on New Years Eve
Full of hopes and promises
For a future we can believe…

A future where all the troubles
Across the world will cease,
A future where all wars will end
Across the bridge of peace…

A future where hope leads to promise
And where love is a beautiful view,
Where faith becomes food for the soul
And where peace is a dream come true.

Always Believe

Welcome your morning
And make positive plans
For you hold your future
In the palm of your hands.

Charter your course
From today where you are,
If you aim for the moon
You can still catch a star.

So always believe
However distant it seems,
You have the power
To fulfill your dreams.

~~~~~o0o~~~~~

Things Will Get Better

These are difficult times we're facing
With the recession biting our heels,
And thousands of people losing their jobs –
They really know how it feels.

It is hard to get up in the morning
With nothing to wear but a frown,
When it seems newspapers are full of bad news
With shop after shop closing down.

But however difficult things may get
There is one thing they can't take away
And that's our ability to hold onto the hope
That things will get better one day.

What a Comforting Thought

What a comforting thought it is

To know that whatever you do,

Your special guardian angel

Is watching over you.

Always there protecting you

Always taking care,

In times of trouble day or night

Your angel is always there.

~~~~~o0o~~~~~

How Brave

How brave the little snowdrop is
To pierce the frozen ground
While bitter winds are blowing
And snow lies deep all around.

And how strong the little snowdrop is
To be fearless and to know
That by sheer determination
It will make it through the snow.

And how proud the little snowdrop is
When it lifts its face to the sun
As if to herald in the spring
Giving hope to everyone.

The Candle of Hope

If you have suffered a recent loss

And you don't know what to do,

When every hour of every day

Is difficult to get through…

Try lighting the candle of hope in your heart

And letting it shine night and day,

Then you will see beyond the clouds

That sunshine is on its way.

~~~~~o0o~~~~~

One Step Ahead

When adversity calls

Be one step ahead

And turn it into

An opportunity instead…

Look for the positive

There is always a chance

Something good can come

From each circumstance.

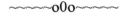

Because I Care

In the chapel of my heart

I quietly said a prayer,

I asked God to send you healing

Because He knows I care.

I sent it on the wings of love

And I know God will have heard,

So just hold onto hope and faith

Because God hears every word

~~~~~~oOo~~~~~~

A Case of Hope

Hope is much like a suitcase
You can fill it full of dreams.
However, if you overload it,
It can burst apart at the seams.

But if your expectations
Are packed within its scope
Your dream will be within your view
While you are holding on to hope.

Hope is the greatest traveller
It can go anywhere with you,
As long as you're holding onto hope
You'll arrive with a dream come true.

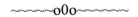

Looking Forward

Keep on looking forward
To the day you hold your dream,
And you will find that nothing is
Quite as bad as it may seem.
Let your determination
Keep a single minded track
Then you will find in the future
There are no tears looking back.

Success can open many doors
Whereas failure opens few,
But you will never fail
As long as you believe in you.
Just keep looking forward
With hope and you will find
It's by far the greatest healer
Of the heart and of the mind.

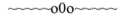

~~~~~oOo~~~~~

Keeping Hope Alive

The human spirit is incredible
And a truly wonderful thing,
Built on a foundation of love
It can endure almost anything.

It can break the chains of oppression
And against all odds survive,
When tossed and torn in troubled seas
It's a light that will keep hope alive.

For the human spirit is remarkable
It will give you the faith to believe,
There is no obstacle you can't overcome
And nothing you cannot achieve.

It's on its Way

I wish I could ease your heartache

And take away your pain,

If I could you know I would

Just to make you feel well again.

But I can send you healing thoughts

And loving wishes to say

I know you will soon feel better

Because hope is on its way.

~~~~~oOo~~~~~

A Second Chance

If you believe you've done your best
Yet somehow failed to pass the test,
Don't let fail become a word
That loses hope each time it's heard.

Reclaim your dream and make a stance
For you deserve a second chance.
There is always another avenue
That faith will find just right for you.

So don't give up, you have the right
To try again and you just might
Find a star that you can pin
All your hopes upon and win…

Aim for the goal within your eyes
And when the time is right you'll win the prize

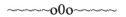

No Prayer Goes Unheard

Across the world thousands were missing
In a quake that would shock and astound,
As people wandered dazed and homeless
A mother prayed her little girl would be found.

Day after day all hope was fading
But then her little girl's voice could be heard
From deep below the dust and rubble -
No prayer goes unheard.

From the ruins of a devastated city
Survivors prayed their cries would be heard,
In a race against time - help was on its way,
No prayer goes unheard...

No Prayer Goes Unheard (continued)

Across the sea floods were raging
As swollen rivers ran deep and wild,
A young woman clung to a tree and prayed,
So afraid and heavy with child.

As rescue came above the torrents
A new born cry could be heard
From within the branches of a tree top -
No prayer goes unheard.

It takes just one lighted candle
Or just one voice to be heard
When praying for a miracle
Because no prayer goes unheard.

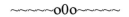

With Love from Me

If I could put hope in a bottle

And cast it out to sea,

I would send it with lots of love

And labelled 'To you, from me'.

For you to find in the sea of life

Whatever the Trade Winds send,

So you will always have hope in your heart

Wherever you go my friend.

If You Believe

There is no broken heart
That cannot be mended
And no problem that cannot be solved.
There is no quarrel
That cannot be ended
And no conflict that can't be resolved.

There is no dream
That cannot be wished for
And no heart that cannot be loved.
There is no peace
That cannot be prayed for
If you believe in the good Lord above.

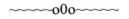

Angels of Hope

Where there is hope
There's a loving smile
And a place to rest
For a little while.

Where there is peace
There is time to pray
For the children of hope today.

Angels of hope
On the wings of a prayer,
Angels of hope
Spreading light everywhere
Angels of hope, angels of love,
Love for children everywhere…

Angels of Hope - *Continued*

Where there is love
There's a hand to care
With a ray of hope
And a dream to share...

So hold onto your dream
Whatever you do
For children of hope
Dreams come true…

Hold onto love
And you will succeed
Because sometimes
Love is all you need.

The Light of Love

If you're going through a tunnel of darkness
And you feel there is no one to care,
When you reach out for a hand to hold
And you're afraid there is no-one there…

Take hold of God's hand in the darkness
His love will show you the way
And you will begin to see clearly
There is hope at the end of the day.

If You Trust Him.

If you've lost direction

And don't know where to start,

Just ask God for guidance –

You'll find Him in your heart.

You won't need a' Sat-Nav'

To help you find your way,

If you trust Him He will get you

Safely through the day.

Your True Value

Everyone is someone
So be proud of yourself,
When you get up in the morning
Don't leave your worth upon the shelf.

Dress yourself in confidence
And remember to wear a smile,
Put your best foot forward
Then face the world in style.

Remember the value you put on yourself
Is the price that someone will pay
To get to know and love you
Because you are someone special today.

~~~~~oOo~~~~~

Because You're Special

You are a very special person,

There is only one of you,

Somewhere there is something

That only you can do…

There is a special corner

Where you can shine your light

And follow your true destiny

On the path you know is right.

Through the Painter's Eyes

He sits there on the hillside
When the sun is hard to find
And paints himself a picture
With the colours in his mind.
He finds a world of sunshine
Far beyond life's cloudy skies,
If only we could see the world
Through the painter's eyes.

The painter paints his people
With a smile on every face,
In their eyes I see depression
But the painter leaves no trace.
He paints a silver lining
Where his visions harmonise,
If only we could see the world
Through the painter's eyes…

The painter paints his children
With his beauty in their eyes,
If their view is overshadowed
By clouds he will improvise.

He paints his faith in colour
For a dream that he can hold,
Such wisdom lies in the painter's eyes
And he's only six years old.

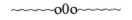

Positive Thinking

I know it can't be easy
To think positive thoughts all the time
When troubles seem to multiply
And none of your reasons rhyme.

But it will only take a moment
To start thinking beautiful things
Like roses in brilliant sunshine
And the feeling of warmth that it brings.

Fill your mind with positive thoughts
And very soon you will find
You will have found the secret
Of a positive heart and mind.

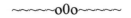

The Miracle of Hope

Hope is such a tiny word

Yet it's used in so many ways,

It's used in times of trouble

And it's used on rainy days.

But when it comes right from the heart

It works hand in hand with love,

For hope and love can work miracles –

With a little help from above.

~~~~~oOo~~~~~

Where There is Hope

If you are searching for a 'Get Well' card
That doesn't have the words 'Get Well'
And you've tried so hard to find a card
With a message the shops don't sell.

Try casting aside your own fears
Even though it may be hard,
Think of all you would wish yourself
And then buy them a 'Get Well' card.

For they will read between the lines
Of a card that does not say
'Get Well Soon' for we all need hope
And to know hope is on its way.

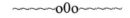

Shades of Hope

God sends us many blessings

Like a moving Kaleidoscope

When life has many twists and turns

To give us shades of hope.

So any time you're feeling troubled

You can give your heart a rest

In the knowledge that God loves you

And that you deserve the best.

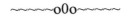

Strands of Hope

If ever you feel troubled
And afraid you cannot cope
It helps to know you can reach out
There are always strands of hope.

It could be that you're just too close
To the problem to clearly see
That in the light of a brand new day
You can view things differently.

For the good Lord never gives you
Any more than you can bear
And it's very comforting to know
When you need Him He is there.

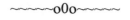

What is Hope?

Hope is an open window

Waiting for the sun to shine.

Hope is the sight of a postman

With the good news you hope to find.

Hope is a dream you hold in your heart

That you pray one day will come true.

Hope is the sight of a sun-kissed dawn

That will always bring hope anew.

~~~~~oOo~~~~~

You Will Go Far

If you have

Hope in your pocket,

Faith in your shoes

and

Love in your heart,

you will travel light

and yet you will go far.

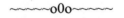

Window of Opportunity

A window is just a window
Until it's opened wide
Where you can get a better view
Of what's on the other side.

It could prove to be a window
Of opportunity -
An opening where you get the chance
To follow your true destiny.

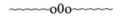

At The End of the Day

Today I lit a candle
For all our heroes who have died
Fighting for their country,
And for all of them I cried.

I prayed for all the broken hearts
That lined the street of tears,
Then I prayed they would find peace
In their hearts for 'stolen years'.

I asked God to hold them in his arms
Until they can make it through
The difficult journey of grief and pride
And to give them hope anew.

The Power of Hope

Faith can move a mountain,

Love can mend a broken heart,

Hope can reach around the world

And still be with you from the start.

Hope is indefinable

And yet we know it is true,

Hope has the power to lift your heart

And to make your dreams come true.

~~~~~oOo~~~~

The Voice of Tomorrow

Children are born free of prejudice-
Just an innocent trust in their eyes,
With a beautiful dream in the making
And not a single cloud in their skies.
Children will never go hungry
If they are fed with a heart full of love,
With plenty of hope and food for the soul
And faith in the good Lord above.

If they are dressed in a coat of confidence
And are given a voice to be heard,
They will become the teachers
And one day will have the last word.
For the children are the voice of tomorrow
And if nurtured today to make plans
To take great care of tomorrow's world
Then our future will be in safe hands.

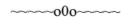

It's Still a Beautiful World

Greet today with hope in your heart

And welcome your morning sun,

Then turn to the page in the book of life

Where the future has just begun.

If you look out across the morning

You'll see it's still a beautiful world,

So welcome the dawn of a brilliant day

And embrace it with both arms unfurled.

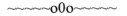

The Price of Love

I know just how you're feeling
I really do understand
What it's like to lose a loved one
And have to let go of their hand.

But hold onto the hope that one day
You will see each other again
In that peaceful place called heaven
Where there is no heartache or pain.

Your tears are part of the grieving
Because tears are the price of love,
But their love will never leave you
Here on earth or in heaven above.

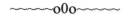

Leaving the Rain Behind

Try to keep looking forward
To new horizons that lie ahead
Don't worry if you've missed the boat,
Something else will come instead.
You have everything to live for
And everything to gain
So step out into the sunshine
And leave behind the rain.

You may have hidden talents
That are about to be unfurled,
So face your day with confidence,
Go out and show the world.
When you've found your confidence
And passed each learning curve,
You will surely be rewarded
With all the happiness you deserve.

~~~~~oOo~~~~~

Behind Every Cloud

Behind every cloud there is a ray of hope

Just waiting there for you,

And behind every cloud there is a dream

Just waiting to come true…

Behind every cloud there is a ray of sun

That shines to help you cope,

So whatever is happening in your world

There is always a ray of hope.

~~~~~o0o~~~~~

The Gift of Hope

We are the caretakers of the world

and our children are the future.

We have something that is within

our gift we can to pass on to them,

and that is 'the gift of hope'…

Hope for a better future.

Hope for a greener world.

Hope for a dream come true,
and
Hope for peace in our time.

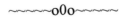

About The Author

Patricia Rose was born in England
and is an accomplished poet who has
had several books of Inspirational verses
published. She is also an award winning
lyricist and songwriter who gains much
of her inspiration from the rich tapestry
of life, and from the many shades of
the human heart.

Her inspiring words offer comfort
and hope in our ever changing world,
for she possesses a wisdom and
spirituality that brings a healing
touch to all her words.

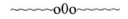